ALFRED's
CRED PERFORMER
COLLECTIONS

How Great Is Our God

MW00826438

Arranged by **Tom Fettke**

12 Popular Praise and Worship Classics

For centuries, God's people have used hymns and gospel songs as vehicles for meaningful praise and worship experiences. In the past three or four decades, new musical forms, commonly called Praise and Worship music, have filled our sanctuaries. They are being sung and played by believers who thirst for a new and vital worship expression. These new songs are a wonderful gift from a God who, without a doubt, loves a variety of musical styles. When used in combination with our rich heritage of powerful hymns and spiritual songs amazing things happen: meaningful, quality musical expressions unite body, soul and spirit in worship of the Living God. *How Great Is Our God* includes twelve of the most effective Praise and Worship songs of our day. In a number of the selections, beloved hymns become part of the arrangements' building blocks—a bit of the old blended with the new. My wish for you is that the word of Christ will dwell in you richly…as you rehearse and perform these psalms, hymns and spiritual songs with gratitude in your hearts to God (Colossians 3:16).

"Antique Clock" photo by Luiz Baltar

Alfred

How Great Is Our God

Words and Music by
Chris Tomlin, Ed Cash and Jesse Reeves
Arr. Tom Fettke

With a sense of awe (♩ = ca.76)

pedal ad lib.

HOLY, HOLY
WITH
HOLY, HOLY, HOLY

Arr. Tom Fettke

Worshipful (♩ = ca. 76)

pedal ad lib.

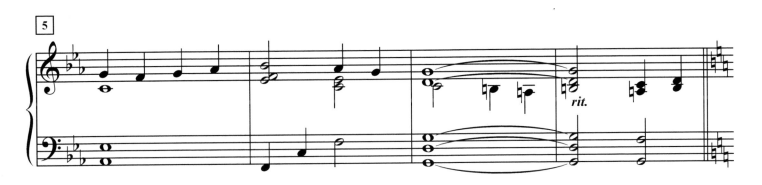

"Holy, Holy"
Words and Music by Jimmy Owens

"Holy, Holy, Holy"
By John B. Dykes

Slowly (♩ = ca. 66)

LAMB OF GOD

Words and Music by Twila Paris
Arr. Tom Fettke

In Christ Alone
(My Hope Is Found)

Words and Music by
Stuart Townend and Keith Getty
Arr. Tom Fettke

SHOUT TO THE NORTH
WITH
RISE UP, O CHURCH OF GOD

Arr. Tom Fettke

"Rise Up, O Church of God"
By Aaron Williams

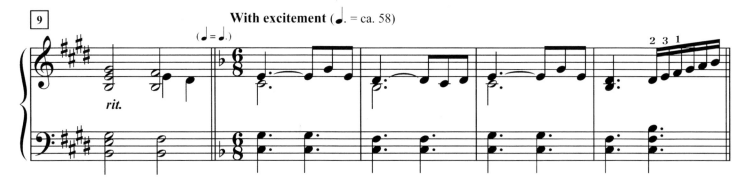

"Shout to the North"
Words and Music by Martin Smith

How Deep the Father's Love for Us

Words and Music by Stuart Townend
Arr. Tom Fettke

Be Still and Know

Arr. Tom Fettke

"Be Still and Know"
Traditional

Freely, with great warmth (♩ = ca.72)

mp

pedal ad lib.

rit.

"Be Still and Know"
Words and Music by Steven Curtis Chapman

Much faster, In Tempo (♩ = ca.116)

mf smoothly

THERE IS A REDEEMER

Words and Music by Melody Green
Arr. Tom Fettke

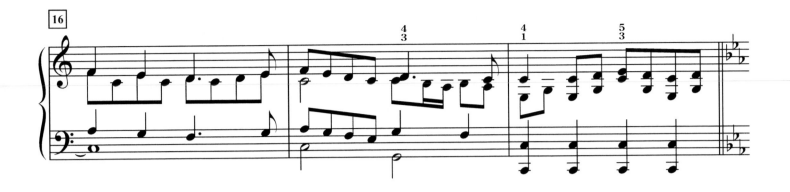

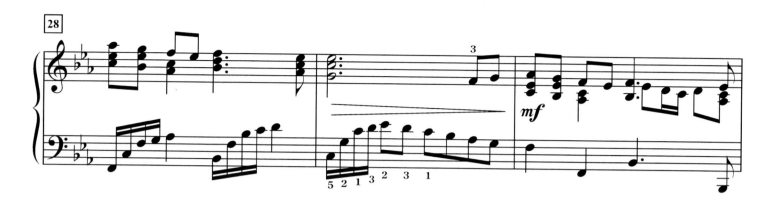

Amazing Grace
(My Chains Are Gone)

Words and Music by Chris Tomlin and Louie Giglio
Incorporating "Amazing Grace" (Traditional American Melody)
Arr. Tom Fettke

Tenderly (♩ = ca. 63)

pedal ad lib.

You Are My King (Amazing Love)
with
And Can It Be?

Arr. Tom Fettke

"You Are My King (Amazing Love)"
Words and Music by Billy James Foote

With adoration (♩ = ca.70)

LH sustained
pedal ad lib.

44

"And Can It Be?"
By Thomas Campbell

ONCE AGAIN
WITH
BENEATH THE CROSS OF JESUS

"Beneath the Cross of Jesus"
By Frederick C. Maker

Arr. Tom Fettke

"Once Again"
Words and Music by Matt Redman

Antiphonal Praise
with
We Have Met to Praise and Worship

Arr. Tom Fettke

With adoration (♩ = ca. 80)

p simply

pedal ad lib.

4

"Antiphonal Praise"
Words and Music by Steve Green

8

12

mp

"We Have Met to Praise and Worship"
By William Moore